Color Your Psalms

An Inspiring Christian Coloring Book for Relaxation, Inspiration and Stress Relief

Scripture Coloring Book with Psalm and

Bible Verse Quote Coloring Pages

This Coloring Book Belongs To

_____

EVEN THOUGH i walk through the DARKEST VALLEY, i will fear no evil, FOR YOU ARE are with me.

PSALM 23:4

Those who look to Him are radiant; their faces are never covered in shame.

PSALM 34:5

He only is my rock and my salvation; he is my defense; I shall not be moved.

PSALM 62:6

He heals the brokenhearted and binds up their wounds

PSALM 147:3

When my heart is faint, lead me to the rock that is higher than I.

PSALM 61:2

For great is your love reaching to the heavens; your faithfulness reaches to the skies.

PSALM 57:10

For He will order his angels to protect you wherever you go.

PSALM 91:11

You are fearfully and wonderfully made.

PSALM 139:14

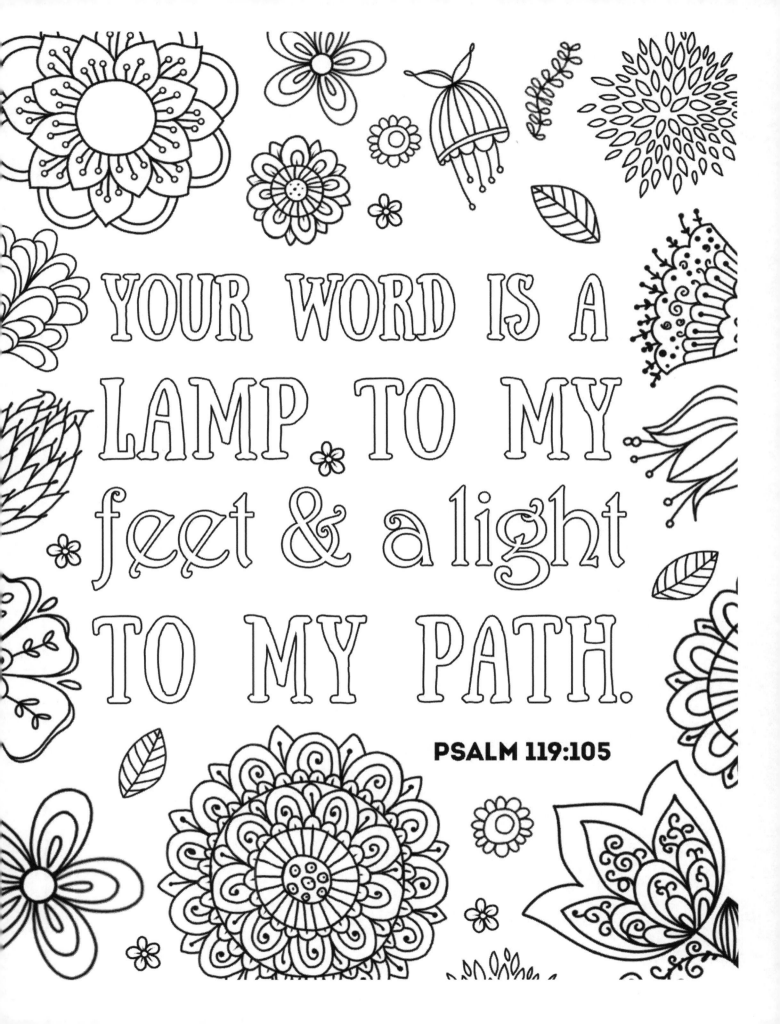

YOUR WORD IS A LAMP TO MY feet & a light TO MY PATH.

PSALM 119:105

I LIFT UP MY EYES TO *the mountains.* WHERE DOES MY HELP COME FROM? *My help comes from the Lord,* THE MAKER OF HEAVEN AND EARTH.

PSALM 121:1-2

Like arrows in the hands of a warrior are children born in one's youth.

PSALM 127:6

Yes, my soul, find rest in God; my hope comes from him.

PSALM 62:5

He is like a tree planted by streams of water that yields its fruit in its season, and its leaf does not wither. In all that he does, he prospers.

PSALM 1:3

YOU ARE THE GOD WHO WORKS WONDERS.

PSALM 77:13-14

Mightier than the waves of the sea is his love for you.

PSALM 93:4

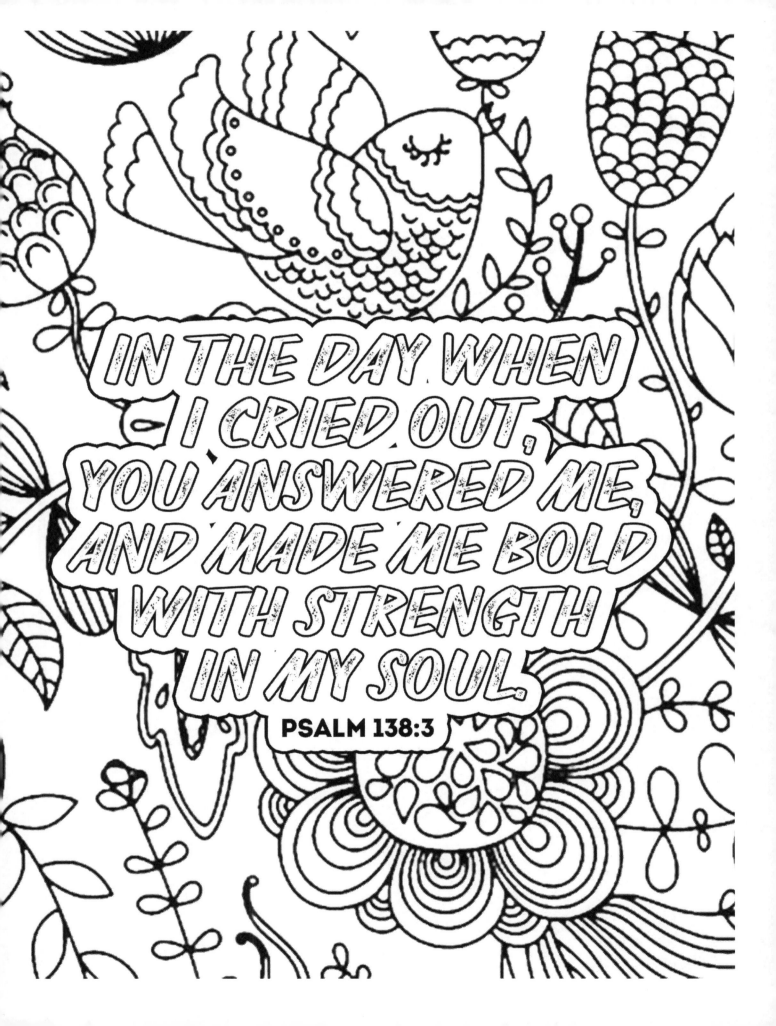

For the Lord takes delight in His people; He crowns the humble with salvation.

PSALM 149:4

He will cover you with his feathers, and under his wings you will find refuge; His faithfulness will be your shield and rampart.

PSALM 91:4

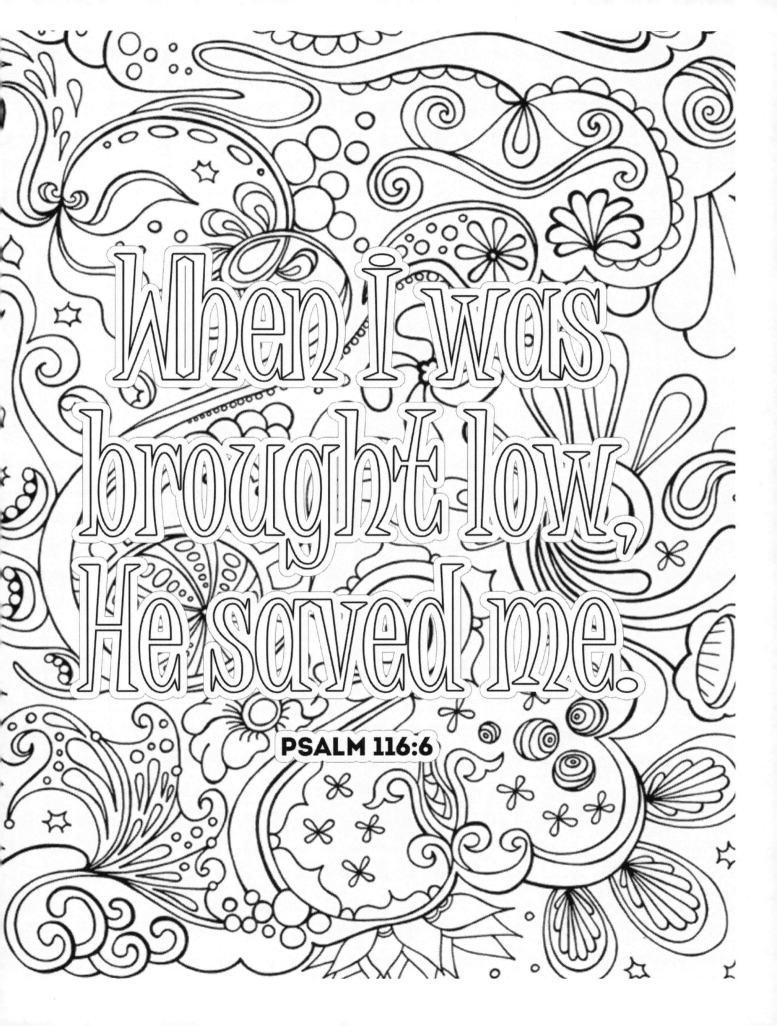

When I was brought low, He saved me.

PSALM 116:6

Under his wings, you will find refuge.

PSALM 91:1

Duplicates

EVEN THOUGH
i walk through the
DARKEST VALLEY,
i will fear no evil,
FOR YOU ARE
are with me.

PSALM 23:4

Those who look to Him are radiant; their faces are never covered in shame.

PSALM 34:5

He only is my rock and my salvation; he is my defense; I shall not be moved.

PSALM 62:6

He heals the brokenhearted and binds up their wounds

PSALM 147:3

When my heart is faint, lead me to the rock that is higher than I.

PSALM 61:2

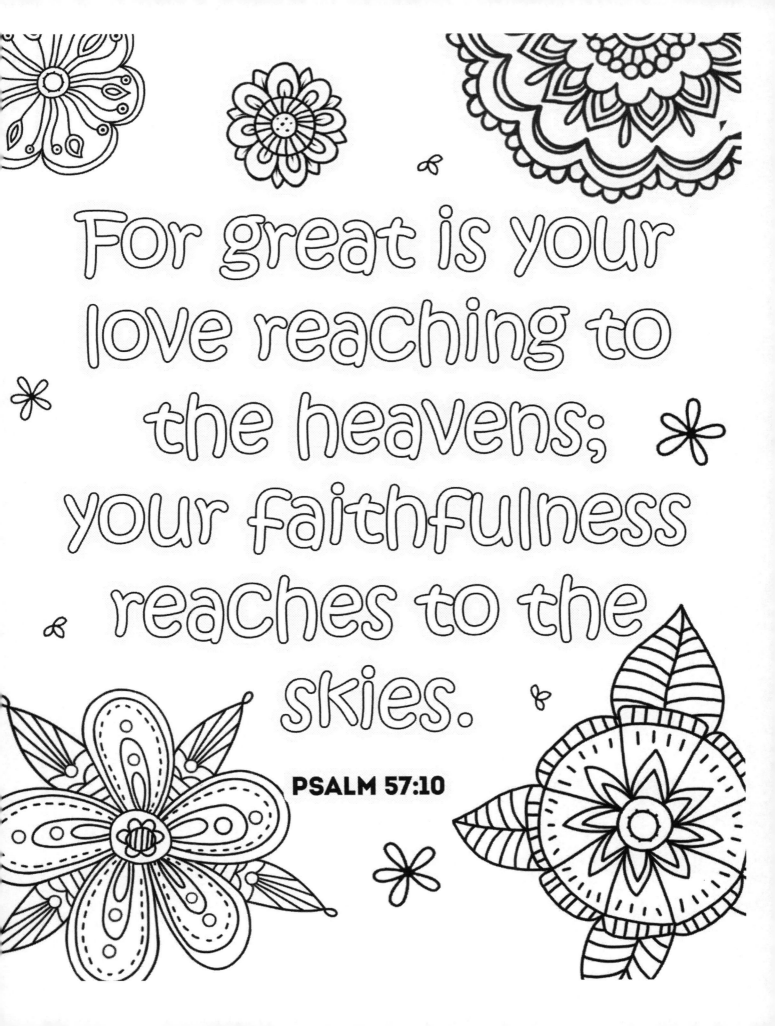

For great is your love reaching to the heavens; your faithfulness reaches to the skies.

PSALM 57:10

Let the morning bring me word of your unfailing LOVE

PSALM 143:8

For He will order his angels to protect you wherever you go.

PSALM 91:11

You are fearfully and wonderfully made.

PSALM 139:14

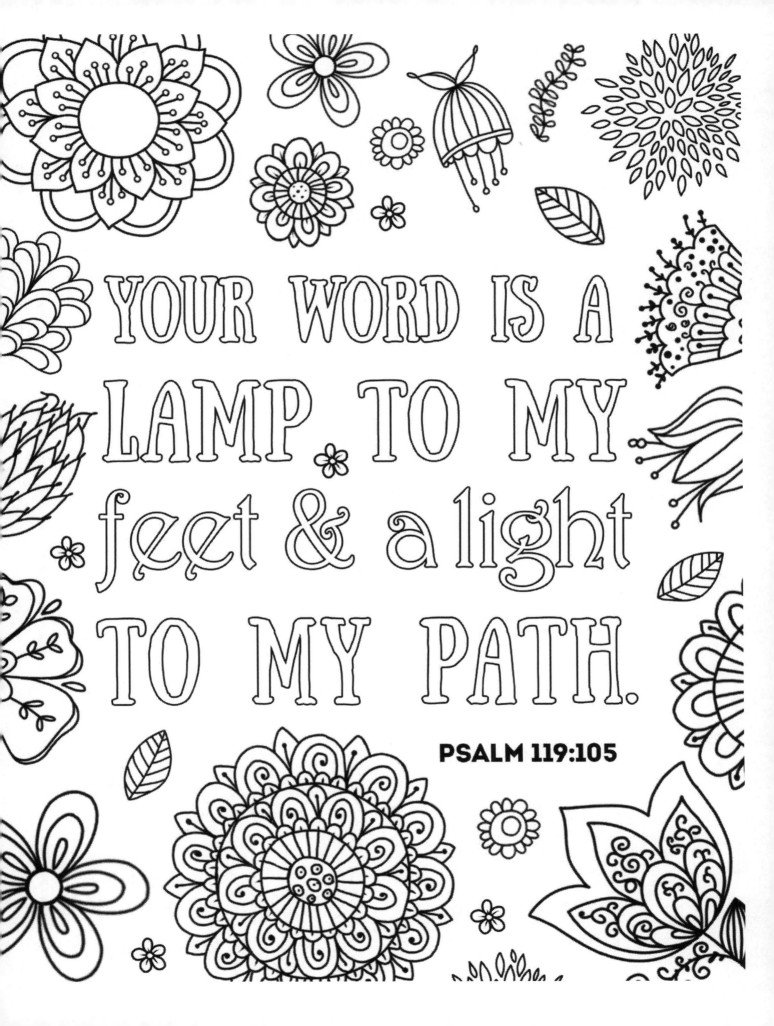

YOUR WORD IS A LAMP TO MY feet & a light TO MY PATH.

PSALM 119:105

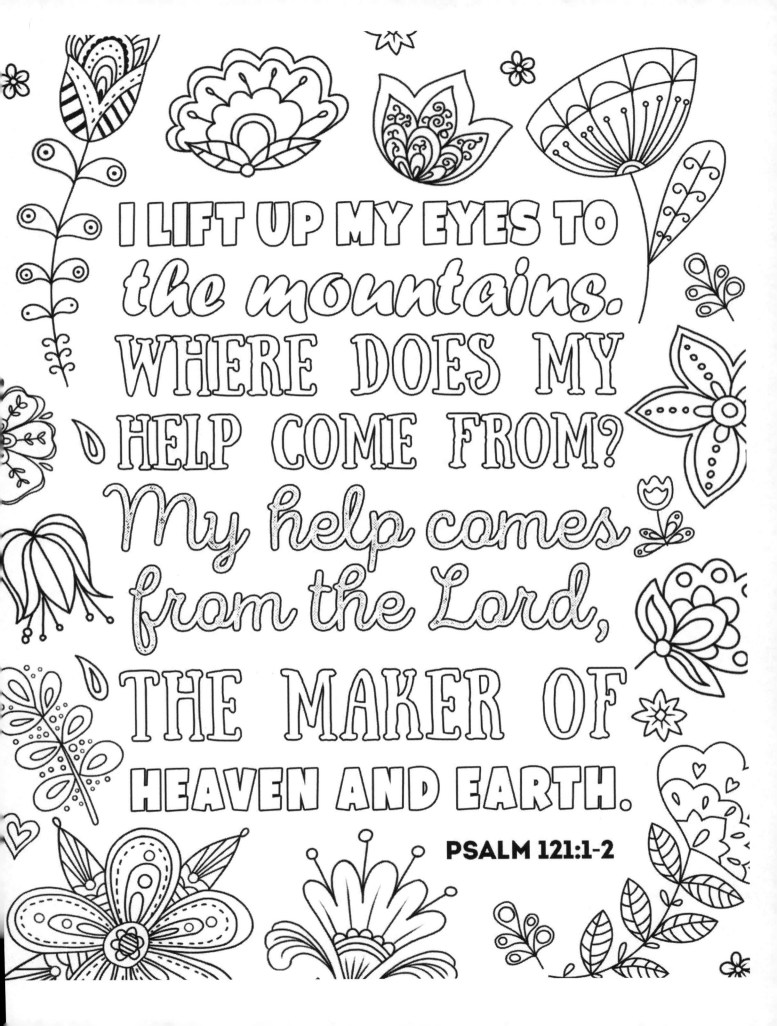

I LIFT UP MY EYES TO the mountains. WHERE DOES MY HELP COME FROM? My help comes from the Lord, THE MAKER OF HEAVEN AND EARTH.

PSALM 121:1-2

Like arrows in the hands of a warrior are children born in one's youth.

PSALM 127:6

Yes, my soul, find rest in God; my hope comes from him.

PSALM 62:5

He is like a tree planted by streams of water that yields its fruit in its season, and its leaf does not wither. In all that he does, he prospers.

PSALM 1:3

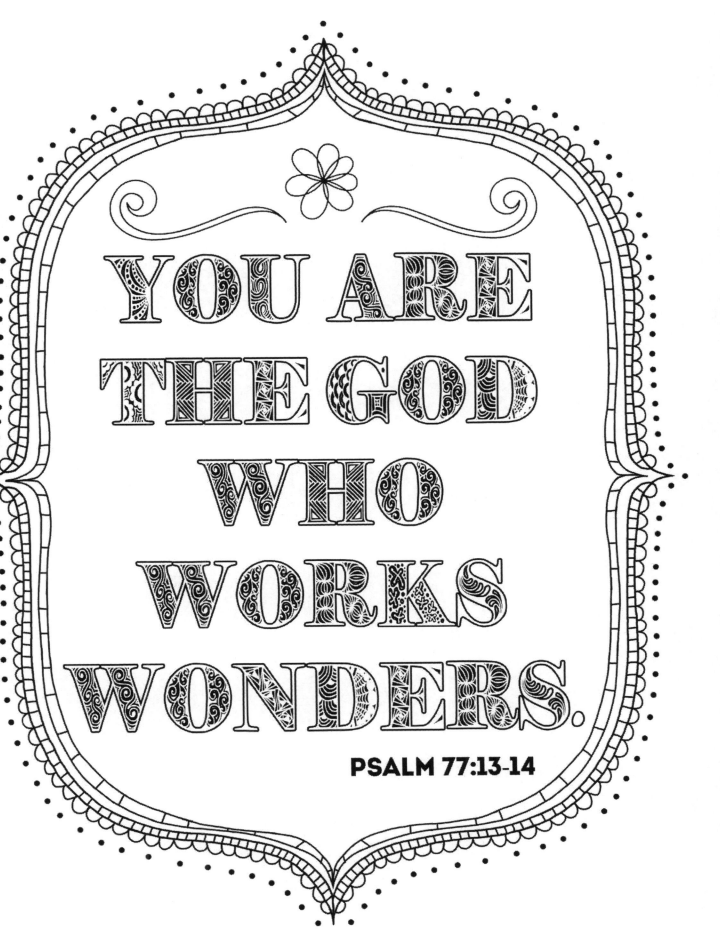

MIGHTIER THAN THE WAVES OF THE SEA IS HIS LOVE FOR YOU.

PSALM 93:4

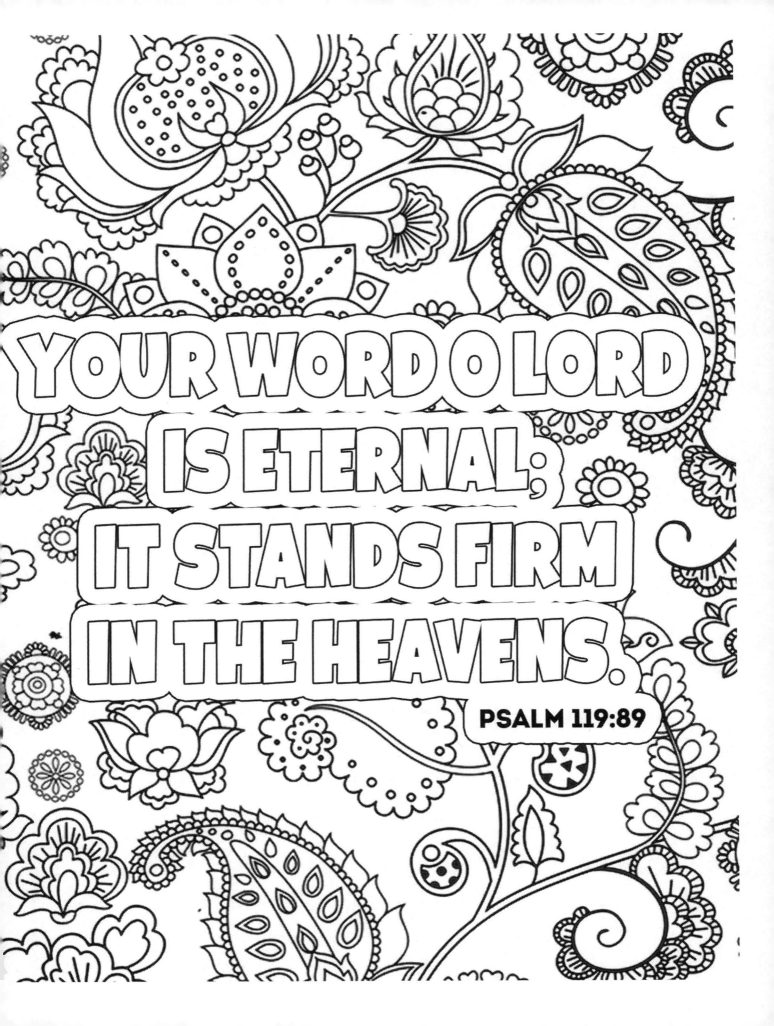

For the Lord takes delight in His people; He crowns the humble with salvation.

PSALM 149:4

MY FLESH & MY HEART MAY FAIL BUT GOD IS THE STRENGTH OF MY HEART & MY PORTION FOREVER.

PSALM 73:26

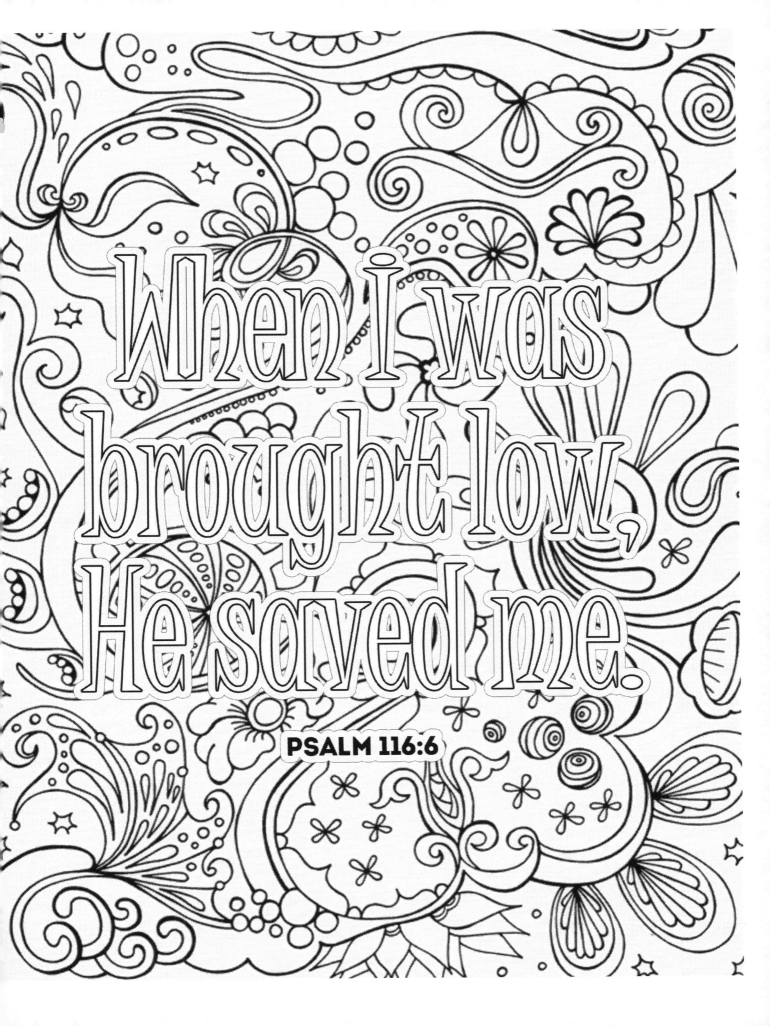

Create in me a clean heart O God and renew a right spirit within me.

PSALM 51:10

Made in the USA
Columbia, SC
25 November 2017